THE MONROE DOCTRINE, 1823

Gathering in Washington, D.C., on December 2, 1823, the members of the Congress of the United States received from President James Monroe his seventh annual State of the Union message. It would prove to be one of the most important ever presented to the Congress, for in it were three paragraphs that would become a keystone of American foreign policy for more than a century. Known today as the Monroe Doctrine, it stated in a general but clear manner both the policy of the United States toward other lands located in the Western Hemisphere and the nation's concern with any attempt to alter the existing political order in the New World.

At the moment of its creation by President Monroe and his secretary of state, John Quincy Adams, it was a brave but dangerous statement for the young and weak American republic to make.

The Monroe Doctrine cautioned the powers of Europe — especially Spain — not to attempt any further colonization or recolonization in the Americas. It explained that since Europe's political system differed from that of America's, the United States would oppose any attempt to bring the former into the Western Hemisphere. It also pledged that the United States would not interfere in the internal affairs of European nations or their existing American colonies, or take part in European wars of solely foreign interest.

The general acclamation received by the Monroe Doctrine told much about the principles of the people and the leaders of the nation who proposed this extraordinary policy in the face of a hostile world.

PRINCIPALS

JAMES MONROE (1758–1831), fifth president of the United States.

JOHN QUINCY ADAMS (1767–1848), secretary of state during the Monroe administrations and sixth president of the United States.

RICHARD RUSH (1780–1859), United States minister to Great Britain, 1817–25.

ALEXANDER I (1777–1825), czar of Russia and author of the Holy Alliance.

FERDINAND VII (1784–1833), reactionary king of Spain, deposed by Napoleon but restored to the throne in 1814.

GEORGE CANNING (1770–1827), British foreign secretary and leader of the House of Commons from 1822 until becoming prime minister in 1827.

SIMON BOLIVAR (1783–1830), most famous of the leaders who freed Latin America from Spain.

PUBLIC ENTRY OF LA FAYETTE INTO NEW YORK

A FOCUS BOOK

The Monroe Doctrine, 1823

A Landmark in American Foreign Policy

by Harold Cecil Vaughan

FRANKLIN WATTS | NEW YORK | LONDON

*Frontispiece: James Monroe,
fifth president of the United States*

Cover photograph shows a part of the Monroe
Doctrine in James Monroe's handwriting. All
photographs courtesy *Charles Phelps Cushing*.

*The authors and publishers of the Focus Books
wish to acknowledge the helpful editorial
suggestions of Professor Richard B. Morris.*

Library of Congress Cataloging in Publication
Data

Vaughan, Harold Cecil.
    The Monroe Doctrine, 1823.

    (A Focus book)
    Bibliography: p.
    1. Monroe doctrine. 2. United States–
Foreign relations. I. Title.
JX1425.V38   327.73   72-8853
ISBN 0-531-02461-X

Contents

Dedicated to my sister
Dorothy Vaughan Brophy

Prologue

Grim indeed was the international scene that faced President James Monroe and the United States when he prepared his lengthy annual message on the State of the Union in December, 1823. The possibility of a war with Spain and its allies in the "Concert of Europe" seemed to draw even closer, as the ninth year since the fall of Napoleon came to an end. Just as disturbing was the realization that even if this war cloud passed by, other disputes with Russia and Great Britain could easily result in conflict.

The root cause of mutual hostility with these great European powers centered primarily around the future of the American continents. Like Africa and most of Asia, the Americas had been looked upon as areas of colonization ever since Spain first planted its flag on the shores of Central and South America in the days of Columbus. The Portuguese, British, French, Swedes, Dutch, and Russians followed the Spanish in laying claim to various parts of the New World. Each in turn then exploited its colonial holdings for the good of the mother country.

For almost three hundred years this pattern of colonization remained intact, disturbed only by the attempts of one or another of the powers to seize the possessions of a rival. Any sort of protest by the original inhabitants of a colony, or even by those who had gone to settle there, was usually ignored, and such uprisings that did occur were ruthlessly suppressed.

Then, to the great surprise of all, came two totally unexpected events that changed the history of the world. The American and French revolutions shattered the old order of things forever. Thirteen of Great Britain's American colonies, with substantial aid from France, won their independence and established a loosely drawn federal republic. Then, in 1789, just two years after the writing of the Constitution of the United States, the great and powerful French monarchy exploded. The principles of republicanism, joined to those of liberty, equality, and fraternity, were carried across Europe by the armies of the new French republic. A shocked Europe quickly ceased its scorn and ridicule of the American experiment, and those who believed in the superiority of a divinely ordained world order were badly shaken.

The wars of the French Revolution and Napoleon kept the Continental powers so busy from 1789 to 1814 that they had little time to concern themselves with events in the Western Hemisphere. For a quarter of a century the United States was able to grow and develop in virtual isolation. Foolishly, in its youthful conceit, it skirted disaster by challenging Great Britain in the War of 1812. Two years later, when peace was reestablished, it had become clear that the United States was no match for the power of Britain, even though the English were still involved with the French in a life-and-death struggle for survival. War weariness and financial exhaustion were the basic reasons for Britain's failure to destroy or even punish severely the American republic.

During the "Era of Good Feeling," which followed the return of peace, Americans tended to act in a more cautious and mature manner. The irresponsible and imperialist cries of the "War Hawks" of 1812, who screamed for the seizure of Canada and promised a quick and easy victory over its British master, were heard no more. The narrow escape from disaster had sobered such men as Henry Clay, John Quincy Adams, and James Monroe. They watched with growing concern the victory of reaction in Europe and the restoration of the old order.

It now seemed logical that the center of world conflict would shift to Latin America. The oppressed peoples in Spain's vast empire had not been immune to the significance of these world-shaking events. Almost fifty years before, they had watched American colonials under British rule win their freedom. When Napoleon had sent an army into Spain in 1807, the tight control the Spanish held over Latin America ended. The king of Spain was forced to abdicate in 1808, and Spanish government officials were so concerned with their own survival that they spent little time in trying to solve the fresh problems arising thousands of miles across the Atlantic Ocean. There, the colonial inhabitants had taken advantage of the power vacuum created by Napoleon. Ignoring or openly defying many of the political and economic restrictions under which they had lived for decades, they moved inexorably closer to the day when they would end forever their colonial status and declare their independence.

This relative isolation, which permitted such freedom of action by the Latin Americans, continued for some time after the final defeat of Napoleon in 1815. The great allied powers of Russia, Austria, Prussia, and Great Britain gave priority to European events before considering the rest of the world. They were bound by the Treaty of Chaumont, signed March 1, 1814, on the eve of Napoleon's downfall. They were also bound by the common aims of reaction and restitution, which dominated the peace settlement negotiated at the Congress of Vienna and were confirmed in November, 1815, by the reactivation of the Quadruple Alliance. It is clear that their main concern was still the possibility of a hostile France.

Not until 1818 were the allied powers satisfied that their recent enemy, now firmly under the rule of the restored Louis XVIII, could be considered a trustworthy member of the Concert of Europe. After a satisfactory congress at Aix-la-Chapelle (the ancient German Rhineland city now called Aachen), the French were permitted to join the Quadruple Alliance, which thus became the Quintuple Alliance.

[3]

The Congress of Vienna, 1815, called to remake Europe after the downfall of Napoleon. Standing to the left in front of his chair is Prince Klemens von Metternich, head of the Austrian government and guiding spirit of the congress.

Reinforcing this military union was a unique document called the Holy Alliance. It was the work of Czar Alexander I of Russia, who believed that military force in this case should be backed by spiritual power. The result was a statement in which the czar, the pious king of Prussia, and the friendly emperor of Austria announced their "fixed resolution, both in the administration of their respective states, and in their political relations with every other government, to take for their sole guide the precepts of that Holy Religion, namely, the precepts of justice, Christian charity, and peace. . . ."

While the czar considered the Holy Alliance a major achievement, few of his less mystical fellow monarchs agreed. Francis I of Austria admitted that he did not know what it meant. Pope Pius VII refused to sign it since it would mean allying himself with the czar, who was the head of a rival (Greek Orthodox) Catholic church. The Sultan of the Ottoman Empire, himself a Muslim, obviously found "Christian" principles unacceptable. Viscount Castlereagh, British foreign secretary, called it "a piece of sublime mysticism and nonsense." Nevertheless, most of the rulers of Europe signed the document, some out of religious conviction and others out of fear of Russia or a need for Alexander's friendship.

Although neither the Quintuple Alliance nor the Holy Alliance was specifically directed against the United States, American leaders feared these alignments might cause trouble. Should conflict with Spain arise, now that Ferdinand VII had been restored to the throne, there was little doubt that he would quickly call for aid from his fellow Christian monarchs. The American experiment with a republican form of government would not inspire friendly feelings in such circles. Neither would the fact that the young nation prided itself on the division of church and state and the disestablishment of the Christian religion. Worse yet, the hated French republic had been inspired by the earlier success of the American experiment, and the United States had warred on Great Britain while that nation was still engaged in destroying Napoleon. Spain, therefore, might expect enthusiastic support for a conflict that could possibly result in the destruction of this American upstart.

President James Madison had worried over the possibility of Spanish intervention in Latin America during the last two years of his administration. So did his secretary of state, James Monroe, who was elected to succeed him in 1816. Yet, half of Monroe's first term passed before the nightmare became a reality.

Thus it was that the New World began in 1818 to ponder with increasing concern the question of whether or not the tide of reaction that had successfully swept across the continent of Europe would now engulf the Americas. Could Spain regain its lost empire? Would Russia, Great Britain, or the United States gain control of the contested lands along the northwest coast of North America? What could the United States do to aid the infant Latin American republics in their struggle to preserve the freedom they had just won? These were some of the questions that President Monroe and his advisers would try to answer.

The Revolt of Spanish America

From the days of Ferdinand and Isabella, when Columbus first planted the Spanish flag in the New World, a vast empire grew and remained virtually intact until the nineteenth century. During those three centuries, the British, French, and Dutch had nibbled away a few islands in the Caribbean, seized a small stretch of Central American coastline, and established claims along the Guiana coast of South America. In all the lands from the vague borders of Florida and Texas to the southern tip of South America, the only colony of any size that did not fly the Spanish flag was the Portuguese settlement in Brazil.

For purposes of administration, the kings of Spain divided these enormous holdings into provinces and districts called viceroyalties and captaincies general. Thus, Mexico became the viceroyalty of New Spain; Ecuador and Colombia the viceroyalty of New Granada; and Argentina the viceroyalty of La Plata. Peru was also accorded this rank. Other areas, such as Chile, Venezuela, Guatemala, and Cuba, held the lesser title of captaincy general.

Spain gave its distant empire little power to govern itself. All important decisions were made by a Council of the Indies, which was appointed by the king and met only in the mother country. Its will was absolute.

In practice, this almost total dictation by king and council proved cumbersome and impossible to enforce on a day-to-day basis. The huge distances that orders had to travel, and even more the lapse of time before they made their uncertain arrival, meant that the viceroy or the captain general, who was physically present in the colony, had to be given tremendous powers. This in turn led to further difficulties. Spain insisted that not only the highest officials, but all judges and lesser administrators, had to be Spanish-born. Only these people, known as *peninsulares*, could govern the empire. Excluded were the *Creoles*, Spaniards born in the colonies; the *mestizos*, people of mixed Spanish and Indian blood; and, of course, the great majority of the inhabitants who were pure Indian.

Still another problem grew out of the Spanish belief in the economic theory called mercantilism. Although refined and labeled by Jean Baptiste Colbert (1619–1683), the financial genius who at a later date served Louis XIV of France, it had actually been practiced by the Spanish since their empire was first founded. Its basic tenet was that the wealth and the power of a nation were based on the possession of precious metals, namely silver and gold. Thus, the Spanish government felt a dependence upon the mines of Mexico and Peru. One-fifth of all the ore taken from the mines went directly to the crown and was chiefly responsible for making Spain the world power it had become.

Mercantilism demanded even more. Colonial industry and commerce were to be discouraged, since without them, the colonies would have to purchase everything they needed from the mother country and to pay for it in gold. Trading with foreign nations was banned so that all purchases would be made directly from Spanish businessmen, thereby bringing still more wealth across the Atlantic to Spain. Such was the theory. But again, actual conditions forced considerable modification. Spain could not always supply the goods needed and wanted by the colonials. Conscious of their monopoly, Spanish merchants often charged unreasonably high prices and provided shoddy and inferior goods. The result was the development of smuggling on a huge scale, despite all the Spanish government's efforts to stop it.

These conditions of colonial exploitation were so brutal and severe that periodically revolt flared. Despite the rapid growth of the number of Spanish-blooded people in the American colonies, they never became strong enough to win any substantial amount of power or freedom. It was estimated that in 1800, Spanish America had over 16,000,000 inhabitants. More than 7,500,000 were Indian, and there were 800,000 blacks, almost all of them slaves. The 5,000,000 mestizos and 3,000,000 Creoles also had reasons to complain against the 300,000 peninsulares, who still held all the highest offices in the government and church, controlled the army, courts, and universities, and dominated the major businesses.

Some of the rebellions called for independence, but most merely demanded reforms. A few were led by Indians, blacks, or mulattoes, but the great majority were led by Creoles, and all were ruthlessly suppressed. Spanish power proved more than sufficient to crush all such upheavals.

The situation began to change about 1800 when an aggressive France, under the brilliant leadership of Napoleon, won domination over an increasingly large part of Europe. The Spanish king, Charles IV, made begrudging concessions to pacify the French, but with little success. He even agreed to cede the vast colony of Louisiana back to France in 1800. However, it was not enough. In 1807 a French army invaded and conquered Spain. The next year Charles IV was forced to abdicate in favor of his twenty-four-year-old son, who became Ferdinand VII. A few months later, when the new king failed to live up to the French emperor's expectations, he was rushed off to exile and imprisonment at the châteu of Valençay in central France. There he would remain for the next five years. Napoleon placed his brother, Joseph Bonaparte, on the throne of Spain.

These events provoked a fierce outburst of nationalism throughout Spain and to some extent in its colonies. Although some of the Spaniards accepted and supported the Bonaparte ruler, most did not. Anti-French patriots soon established a Council of the Regency, which in turn called a *cortes* (parliament) and organized, with increasing aid from the British, opposition to French rule in the name of the imprisoned Ferdinand VII.

A parallel course of action could be seen in many of the colonies, where local leaders supported the insurgents in Spain. They refused to obey orders from Joseph Bonaparte. They justified home rule or autonomy by each of the colonies until such time as the Spanish king was freed. They argued that the empire was Ferdinand's private possession not Spain's, and so they absolved themselves of any obedience to any government in the mother country. Even when the regency and cortes attempted to assert their will and authority, they were met with the same arguments from the colonies. In fact, although not in theory, most of the colonies had seized power for themselves. With each passing year, the chances that the colonies would return it voluntarily, even to a restored king, became increasingly remote.

All of these extraordinary events were watched for years by a Creole named Francisco Miranda (1750?–1816). Early in his life he dedicated himself to the cause of independence for Spanish America. His military training had begun in the Spanish army from 1773 to 1782. Then he joined the French army in the early days of the Revolution and rose to the rank of general, commanding a division under the great French general Charles Dumouriez. Later he moved on to England and the United States. He encouraged secret revolutionary societies, which he had helped to found as early as the 1780's, and pleaded the cause of freedom to various foreign governments from whom he sought aid. By 1806 he was ready. An expedition left New York City for his native

Joseph Bonaparte was placed on the throne of Spain by his brother.

land, the captaincy general of Caracas (Venezuela), where it was promptly defeated. So was a British invasion of the viceroyalty of La Plata (Argentina), begun the same year.

Miranda, in despair, resumed his operations in London for another two years. Not until 1810 had the situation improved enough for him to return once more to Venezuela. By then the leaders of the captaincy general had refused to recognize Joseph Bonaparte as king, had established a provisional administrative junta (council), had deposed the captain general, had repudiated the regency, cortes, and Ferdinand VII, and finally declared independence.

As it turned out, Miranda, now in his sixties, would soon be challenged as the champion of those who supported independence. Another Creole, Simón Bolívar (1783–1830), appeared in London as the representative of the Venezuelan junta. Seeking the support of the British government, he met and allied himself with Miranda. In December, 1810, the plans to return home were complete, and both men sailed separately, the twenty-seven-year-old Bolívar arriving several days before Miranda. Both were quickly engaged by the royalist forces under the command of General Domingo de Monteverde. Early victories were followed by defeats, after an earthquake that seemed to strike only at those strongholds held by the republicans. Morale collapsed, and Miranda capitulated on July 25, 1812. Bolívar and other rebel leaders were dismayed at what they considered a virtual betrayal of the cause. Miranda was arrested and later allowed to fall into the hands of the royalists. He was sent back to Spain and died in a prison in Cádiz four years later.

Bolívar escaped to the city of Cartagena in New Granada

Simón Bolívar, known as the Liberator and often called the "George Washington of South America"

(Colombia), where he raised a small army. In August, 1813, he regained Caracas and won for himself the title "El Liberator." But the struggle was far from over, for shortly thereafter he faced a new royalist army under the command of José Tomás Boves. By the end of 1814 Boves was victorious; all of Venezuela except the island of Margarita had been recaptured; and Bolívar once again fled to Cartagena. From there he moved to Jamaica and finally to Haiti. Not until 1815 did he return to Venezuela to begin the final campaign. It then took three more years before victory was won, and all of New Granada and the captaincy general of Caracas were permanently freed.

Meanwhile, at the southern end of South America, another hero of the independence movement was active. José de San Martín (1778–1850), the son of a Creole mother and a peninsular father, had risen to power.

Five years older than Bolívar, San Martín was born in Yapeyú (now in Argentina) on the Uruguay River. At the age of eight his family moved to Spain where he soon began to train for a military career. Before his return to America in 1812 he had fought in campaigns against the Moors in North Africa, the English, the Portuguese, and the French. Meanwhile, back in La Plata, patriotic colonials had repulsed a British invasion in 1806 with no help from Spain. Support for independence grew, and by 1810, when news of Napoleon's almost total defeat of the royalists reached Buenos Aires, the viceroy was deposed and a provisional junta assumed control of the "Provinces of the Plata River."

San Martín joined the rebel forces upon his return, and in 1814 was made governor of the province of Cuyo. There in the foothills of the Andes he spent two years planning for the liberation of Chile and Peru from Spanish rule. Slowly he raised and equipped an army of 5,500 men. To avoid the mistakes made by

Bernardo O'Higgins, who had almost won freedom for Chile years before, only to suffer final defeat in 1814, San Martín prepared carefully for the difficult passage across the Andes. He planned well. When his tiny army reached Chile, it quickly won its first major battle at Chacabuco. Two days later, on February 14, 1817, he occupied the capital city of Santiago.

The struggle then shifted to coastal waters. Two years were required to amass a navy large enough to drive the royalists from the area. Some ships were captured by the rebels. Others were purchased with the help of funds from British and American interests. They believed that independence would ultimately allow them entrance into the profitable markets of South America, which up to this time had been restricted to Spanish merchants and businessmen.

With Chile secured, the rebel forces moved north toward Peru. Liberation came slowly, but by 1821 the capital of Lima was freed, and San Martín's dream had become a reality.

Similar stories could be told about other sections of Spanish America. Paraguay was liberated as early as 1811. The Dominican Republic was formed in 1844. The viceroyalty of New Spain (Mexico) saw an unsuccessful uprising led by Indian Catholic priests Miguel Hidalgo and José María Morelos in 1810. Eleven years later, Augustín de Iturbide, an ex-officer in the Spanish army, led a more conservative revolt. It resulted in the birth of an empire, which included Guatemala and all of Central America. A year later, however, in 1823, Emperor Iturbide was overthrown by a more radical revolution, ending in his death and the creation of a separate Central American union. Mexico itself became a republic.

Although the details of each of these liberation movements varied, as did the amount of time needed to gain freedom from Spain, one characteristic reaction was true in every case. The winning of independence by each colony was welcomed by both

CARIBBEAN SEA

ATLANTIC OCEAN

Barranquilla
Morón
Valencia ★ La Guaíra
Maracaibo ★ Caracas
VENEZUELA
Orinoco R.
Georgetown
GUYANA
SURINAM
Paramaribo
DEVIL'S ISLAND
FR. GUIANA
Cayenne

Medellín
Bogotá
Buenaventura
Cali
COLOMBIA
Popayán
Cerro Bolívar
GUIANA HIGHLANDS

EQUATOR

Otavalo
ECUADOR ★ Quito
Guayas River
Guayaquil

Japurá R.
Rio Negro
River
Pará R.
Belém

Manaus
Amazon
River

Iquitos
Javari R.
Juruá
River
River
River
River
São Francisco River
Recife

Chan Chan

PAN AMERICAN
PERU
Purus
River
Madeira River
BRAZIL
Tapajós
Xingu
Araguaia River

Lima
HIGHWAY
Cuzco
Lake Titicaca
La Paz
Tiahuanaco
BOLIVIA
Santa Cruz
Sucre
Brasília
Salvador (Bahia)

Potosí

ATACAMA DESERT

A N D E S

GRAN CHACO
Paraguay R.
PARAGUAY
Paraná
Belo Horizonte
Ouro Prêto
Volta Redonda
São Paulo
Rio de Janeiro

Asunción
Tucumán
A R G E N T I N A
Paraná
Blumenau
Joinvile

Mt. Aconcagua
PAMPAS
Uruguay
Porto Alegre

Valparaíso
Mendoza
Santiago
Buenos Aires
URUGUAY
Montevideo
River Plate

CHILE
Concepción
Río Colorado

N

South America

0   50   100
Miles
EQUATOR
GALÁPAGOS ISLANDS

PACIFIC OCEAN

PATAGONIA

Strait of Magellan
Ushuaia
TIERRA DEL FUEGO
Cape Horn

FALKLAND ISLS.

Iguassu Falls

0   200   400   600   800   1000
Miles

BUCTEL

Great Britain and the United States. These two nations looked forward to an increasingly profitable commercial relationship with the new countries of Latin America. For Americans there was the added satisfaction of seeing new republics born. Although liberal only by comparison with the reactionary governments of Europe, they reinforced the beliefs held in the United States that the republican form of government was not unique to former British colonies alone. Reactionary monarchies might have regained control of most of Europe, but that did not appear to be what the future would hold for the nations of the New World.

In his annual message to Congress in December, 1823, President Monroe defended the rights of the independent Latin American nations. By then they included almost all of what, but a few years before, had been the seemingly indestructable empire of the king of Spain.

Through the efforts of men like Bolívar and San Martín, the former Spanish colonies became the independent South American countries of today.

[17]

United States
Relations
with Spain

American foreign policy today is concerned with every corner
of the globe, and there is not a nation unaffected by decisions
made in Washington. But in the early nineteenth century, such
was not the case. In those days the United States awaited decisions
made by other powers and had relatively little to do with much
of the world. To speak of American foreign relations in that
period was to discuss almost exclusively dealings with Great
Britain, France, and Spain.

Relations with the Spanish had rarely been good. As part of
the British Empire, the thirteen American colonies had played a
role in the great rivalry, then several centuries old, between Great
Britain and Spain. Queen Elizabeth's defeat of the Spanish Armada
was part of the colonies' heritage. So was their Protestant faith,
which in an age still marked by great religious intolerance bred
fear and hatred toward the most Catholic of all the powers of
Europe. Spanish possessions in North America caused additional
friction.

Florida had been claimed by Spain in 1513, a century before
the first Englishmen appeared in Virginia. In the seventeenth century, however, as British settlements quickly expanded, border
disputes developed. Georgia, the southernmost British colony, was
settled in 1732, partly to act as a buffer between the Carolinas and
Spanish Florida. It is true that the troublesome Florida peninsula
became a British colony at the close of the French and Indian War
in 1763, but this situation only lasted for twenty years. In the

peace settlement that ended the American Revolution, Florida was returned to Spain.

The newly formed United States was hardly in a position to protest the transfer since, during the recent war, they had been fighting on the same side as the Spanish. Not that the government in Madrid had discovered a hidden passion for the American rebels. Rather, the Spanish had been talked into the American Revolution by their French neighbors, who desired assistance against the British and who were quick to point out that the war provided an excellent opportunity for Spain to regain Gibraltar. At the peace table in 1783, however, things worked out differently. The peninsula that Spain regained proved to be Florida rather than Gibraltar.

Insufficient exploration, inadequate mapping of the common border, and conflicting claims of ownership were true not only in the case of Florida, but for the western frontier of the new republic as well. There the treaty stated that the Mississippi River would be the dividing line between the United States and the enormous Spanish colony of Louisiana. At that time, however, the actual course of the river was not fully known. Worse yet from the American point of view, Spain possessed both banks of the lower river, along with the great port city of New Orleans. Since most of the trade and commerce of the western part of the United States used the Mississippi and its tributaries as a natural highway through the wilderness, it seemed unbearable to many Americans that the river mouth and its key port should belong to a foreign power. For twenty years this problem grew in importance as the population of such western states as Kentucky and Tennessee increased and trade expanded.

Suddenly the situation became critical. In 1800 Napoleon forced Spain to cede Louisiana to France. At this point he had plans to reestablish a great French Empire in North America. Events during the next two years, however, destroyed this dream. A successful revolt by black slaves on Hispaniola, and the destruction of a French army sent to crush it, ended any hope of using the island as an intermediate base between France and Louisiana. Napoleon also feared that once the cession became known (the Spanish flag flew over Louisiana for almost three years after it had become a French possession), the British might try to seize it as a prize of war. While it is true that almost ten years of fighting between France and England ended with a treaty signed on March 25, 1802, Napoleon suspected that the truce would only be temporary. Ten months later he himself would end it and resume the struggle, which ceased only when he was destroyed. Slowly but realistically he faced the facts. Once war began, the British navy, which controlled the Atlantic Ocean, would cut France off from Louisiana. Then most likely an American or a British army would seize the defenseless colony.

Meanwhile, news of the secret transfer was spreading. As early as 1801 rumors of the cession had begun to circulate in New Orleans, and the next year President Thomas Jefferson learned that they were true. The United States now had a new and far more powerful neighbor than Spain on its western border. At the beginning of 1803 Jefferson appointed James Monroe as a special envoy to France. He was to assist Robert R. Livingston, the United States minister in Paris, to negotiate the purchase of the New Orleans area and West Florida. (Jefferson assumed that West Florida had also been transferred to France.) Then suddenly Napoleon astonished Livingston by offering to sell all of Louisiana to the United States. Although not authorized to do so, Livingston accepted the incredible offer. When Monroe arrived, he, too,

The Louisiana Purchase, 1803, doubled the nation's size.

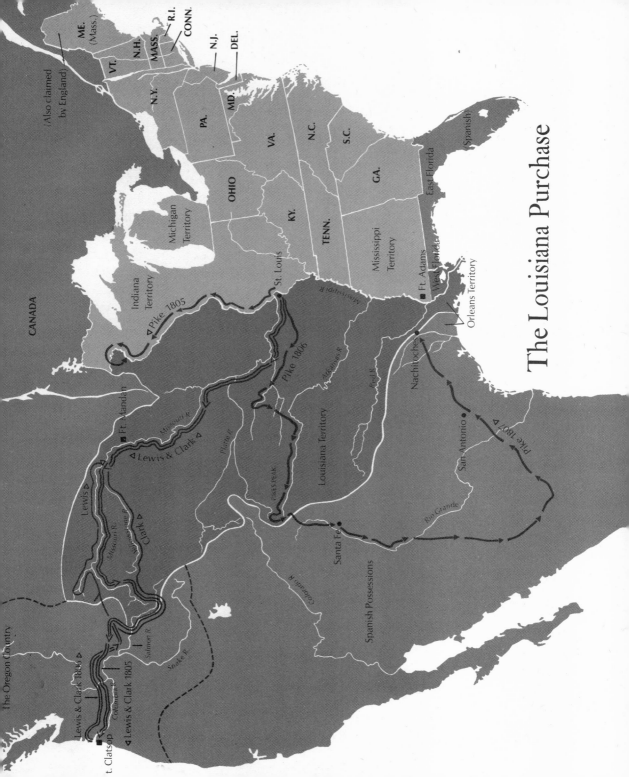

The Louisiana Purchase

CANADA

(Also claimed by England)

ME.
(Mass.)

VT.
N.H.
MASS.
R.I.
CONN.
N.Y.
N.J.
DEL.
PA.
MD.
VA.
N.C.
S.C.
GA.
OHIO
KY.
TENN.
Mississippi Territory
Michigan Territory
Indiana Territory

The Oregon Country

Lewis & Clark 1805
Lewis & Clark 1805
Lewis
Clark
Lewis & Clark
Columbia R.
Salmon R.
Snake R.
Missouri R.
Missouri R.
Platte R.
Pike 1805
Pike 1806
PiKES PEAK
Ft. Mandan
St. Louis
Mississippi R.
Arkansas R.
Red R.
Louisiana Territory
Santa Fe
San Antonio
Rio Grande
Colorado R.
Spanish Possessions
Nachitoches
Pike 1807
Ft. Adams
West Florida
Orleans Territory
East Florida
(Spanish)
t. Clatsop

endorsed the proposal. In the treaty signed in May, 1803, the United States agreed to pay about fifteen million dollars for an area that doubled the nation's size!

This major shift in the political and territorial makeup of North America increased rather than diminished friction between the United States and Spain. Although the troublesome Mississippi border was gone, and the Stars and Stripes flew over New Orleans, a new and almost nonexistent border promised more trouble at a future date. Vague lines on inaccurate maps pretended to separate the western border of Louisiana from the Texas, New Mexico, and California regions, all of which were then part of the viceroyalty of New Spain (Mexico).

Of even more immediate concern was the question of West Florida. In the Treaty of San Lorenzo, negotiated in 1795 by Thomas Pinckney, Spain admitted to United States ownership of the disputed area north of thirty-one degrees latitude. The territory south of that line was claimed by Spain, thus cutting off Americans in Mississippi and Alabama from the Gulf of Mexico. Jefferson claimed that this strip of coastline, which ran from the Mississippi just north of New Orleans eastward to the Apalachicola River, was included in the purchase of Louisiana. Both Napoleon and the Spanish government denied the claim.

Some years later, in 1810, President James Madison took advantage of a revolt against Spanish rule in the area. He ordered the occupation of the section running eastward from the Mississippi River to the Perdido River and proclaimed it part of the United States. Half of it was attached to the territory of Orleans, and in 1813 the remainder was incorporated into the Mississippi Territory.

To the dismay of most Americans living in the South, a third of West Florida and all of East Florida was left in Spanish hands.

They saw the entire area as a badly administered refuge for hostile Indians, pirates, and runaway slaves. President Madison and the government could do little about the situation during the battle with Great Britain in the War of 1812, but upon its conclusion in 1815, demands for annexation were heard once more.

By 1817 a new President, James Monroe, and his secretary of state, John Quincy Adams, were pointing out to Ferdinand VII that his nation at various times in the past few decades had destroyed American goods and ships. Spain had also permitted British forces to operate in Florida and had failed to curb the criminal activities of Indians and others operating out of Florida bases against Americans across the border. In payment for these and other damages, it was suggested that all of Spanish Florida be ceded to the United States. In addition, Spain must permit the drawing of a definite boundary line, ending the conflicting claims to territories beyond the Mississippi.

Ferdinand VII and Don Luis de Onís, his minister in Washington, ignored these demands or at least refused to complete negotiations, which dragged on interminably. Frustrated, the Americans even considered breaking off the talks; their fear, however, that if war came the British might come to the aid of Spain, persuaded them to continue. But nothing was achieved, and war nearly did break out. The fiery commander of the southern military district, General Andrew Jackson, invaded Florida on March 10, 1818!

A typical westerner of the time who hated Indian and Spaniard alike, Jackson had called upon his superiors for permission to act ever since the Seminole Indians had raided across the border in 1817. The government did agree to allow future Indian raiders to be pursued back into Spanish territory and there destroyed, provided they did not take refuge in a Spanish post. General Jackson ignored the limitations placed on this policy, as perhaps President Monroe and Secretary of War John C. Calhoun hoped he would.

With seventeen hundred men and no immediate provocation, Jackson plunged into the rainy swampland of Florida. Five days later he forced the surrender of the Spanish garrison at St. Marks. No Indians had been captured, but Jackson did seize Alexander Arbuthnot, a British subject who traded with the Indians and was known to be a friend of the Seminoles. The army then advanced 200 miles farther down the peninsula, aiming at the Indian village of a chief named Boleck. When they arrived on April 18 the village was virtually empty. Two Indians and nine blacks were killed. That night Robert Ambrister, an Englishman, was captured. He carried papers indicating that he had warned the Indians of the approaching American force. Later other documents were discovered that proved Arbuthnot had done the same. Jackson then returned to St. Marks where he put both prisoners on trial. On April 29, 1818, Arbuthnot was found guilty of spying and inciting the Indians to war and was hanged. Ambrister was found guilty of leading the Indians to war on the United States and was hanged. The general then pushed on into West Florida and laid siege to Pensacola and its fort, which fell after a minor skirmish on May 28, 1818.

By mid-June word of Jackson's activities reached Washington. The Spanish and British ministers raged. President Monroe and his cabinet were horrified at the thought that another war was at hand. A three-day cabinet meeting began on July 8. It was unanimously agreed that the captured forts be returned to Spanish authorities. Monroe and Calhoun were also ready to repudiate Jackson and bring him home in disgrace, but at this point he was defended by Secretary of State Adams. The general received a simple reprimand. Adams also reassured his colleagues that no war would result over these events. He felt that Spain was too weak to fight, and the British would not consider the execution of two of their subjects important enough. Adams proved correct on both accounts. Indeed, when word did come from Madrid to Minister Onís, it instructed him to end his delaying tactics and settle with the Americans.

By February, 1819, less than a month after Onís had heard from Ferdinand VII, the treaty was complete. Spain renounced all claims to East Florida, West Florida, and Louisiana. The agreement also set down, on grossly inaccurate maps, the new western boundary of the United States. Spain gave up any right it had to land north of the forty-second parallel, from the Rocky Mountains to the Pacific, thus dropping out of the contest for Oregon. The boundary line from the Rockies to the Gulf of Mexico was set along the west bank of the Arkansas, the Red, and the Sabine rivers and connecting meridians of longitude. In return the United States assumed five million dollars' worth of Spanish debts owed to American merchants and shipowners. It was a brilliant triumph of American diplomacy and even more of the genius of John Quincy Adams.

Any hope that friendlier relations between Spain and the United States might now develop proved false. The Florida problem had been solved, but most Americans remained hostile. Their full attention now turned toward the infant nations of Latin America. From the beginning, the people of the United States had felt enormous sympathy with the Spanish colonies as they fought their way to freedom. Some of the most persuasive statesmen of the times, such as Henry Clay, were early champions of their cause, seeing in the struggle a repetition of America's own battle for independence and the right to establish a republican form of government. The only question that might divide the citizens of the United States was the degree to which their nation should go in supporting these weak states against the enemies who plotted their destruction.

Now, even before the Florida treaty was a year old — and as yet unsigned by the principals — Ferdinand VII was busy gathering a fleet and army at the port of Cádiz in southern Spain in an effort to reconquer and subdue his Latin American empire. Once more a major clash of policy between the two nations seemed imminent. Only the revolt of the Spanish people and the mutiny of the army against their reactionary king prevented the fleet from sailing. The revolutionary government that seized power forced the king to accept the liberal constitution that had been written in 1812 and to sign the Adams-Onís Treaty. Some months later it was ratified by the United States Senate and was proclaimed on February 13, 1821.

Although the unscrupulous and vindictive despot Ferdinand VII had suffered a setback, he was soon active again, planting seeds of dissension among his opponents at home and appealing for aid from the other Continental powers. His problems were considered, over British objections, by Prince Klemens von Metternich, head of the Austrian government, and the Concert of Powers at a congress held in Verona, Italy, in 1822. There Spanish representatives met with those from Great Britain, Russia, Prussia, Austria, and France. With Britain alone refusing to agree, it was decided to take action. Proclaiming in exaggerated fashion what were described as conditions of anarchy in Spain, the congress demanded the abolution of the constitution of 1812 and the king's return to power. When the liberals refused, the congress went

Above: General Andrew Jackson meeting with Indian chief William Weatherford
Below: Ferdinand VII of Spain appealed for aid from other continental powers.

[26]

further. A French army under the Duke of Angoulême, nephew of Louis XVIII, was ordered to invade Spain. By October, 1823, the badly organized and defeated liberals again listened to the blandishments of Ferdinand, and laid down their arms. His promises of a general pardon and moderate rule were soon forgotten, and the repression of 1824 would prove even more cruel than that of 1814.

As 1823 ended, Ferdinand was once again in a position to turn his eyes toward the still unpunished rebels in distant America. However, the years of delay from 1819 to 1823 had altered the situation. The attitude of the independent states of Central and South America had now passed the point of no return. No longer were they willing to submit to the rule of Spain in return for the granting of a few concessions. Furthermore, the United States, under the leadership of President Monroe, had faced the problem squarely and had taken a stand. At the President's request, the Congress of the United States, in March, 1822, granted recognition to the former Spanish colonies that had declared their independence. The list included Argentina, Greater Colombia (then including Venezuela), Chile, Peru (where the struggle would continue for two more years), and the recently proclaimed Republic of Mexico. No other power had granted such recognition. Clearly the independent states throughout the Americas could now count on the assistance of the United States if they chose to fight to maintain their freedom.

The Russian Threat

President Monroe and the majority of Americans concerned with foreign policy in the early 1820's considered Spain's attempt to regain its former colonies as the chief threat to the peace and security of the New World. They also realized that, without the aid and assistance of the reactionary rulers of the great Continental powers, Ferdinand's threat would be a minor one. Louis XVIII of France, Frederick William III of Prussia, Francis I of Austria, and Alexander I of Russia had differences among themselves, but all were firmly united in their dedication to the principles of absolute monarchy, their hatred of republicanism, and their fear of revolution. They had combined to defeat Napoleon in 1814, and in the postwar period had allied themselves militarily in the so-called Quadruple-Quintuple Alliance and spiritually in the Holy Alliance.

As the strongest member of the reactionary nations supporting Spain, Russia was looked upon with suspicion by the United States. This distrust and hostility was reinforced by a more direct challenge by the Russians. At that time the far distant Pacific coast was not considered as vital to America's future as Latin America. Nevertheless, any expansion of Russian-held Alaska did cause some concern in Washington, even though the United States had only the vaguest of legal claims to any part of the area.

Russian penetration of North America dated back to the famous Danish navigator Vitus Bering (1680–1741). In 1728 he discovered the straits that separate Siberia from Alaska and now bear his name. Thirteen years later he explored the Alaskan coastline around the fifty-eighth parallel. Fur traders and fishermen soon followed, as did the founding of trading posts. On July 8, 1799, the Russian-American Fur Company was chartered by Czar

Paul I and was granted jurisdiction as far south as the fifty-fifth parallel (currently the southern border of Alaska). Expansion continued, however, and on September 11, 1812, the Russians established Fort Ross (actually Fort Rossiya, an ancient name for Russia) some 13 miles north of Bodega Bay, which they claimed, and only 80 miles north of San Francisco.

Three nations contested Russia's claims to the north Pacific coast. Although Spain maintained that the northern boundary of its California colony stretched all the way from Mexico to the sixty-first parallel, no settlements had been made north of the San Francisco area, so there was little serious possibility of a clash with the Russians. Moreover, in the Florida treaty of 1819 Spain agreed to reduce its claims and accept a new northern boundary along the forty-second parallel (currently the California-Oregon border).

The second nation involved was Great Britain. Based on the voyage of Sir Francis Drake in the *Golden Hind* in 1579 and on the mapping activities of Captain James Cook in 1778, the British laid claim to the whole indefinite area between Alaska and California, which came to be known as Oregon.

By far the weakest claim to the Pacific coast of North America was held by the United States, for not until 1803 and the Louisiana Purchase did its territory even approach the western ocean. Then, with the American border snaking through the inland peaks of the Rockies, Americans began looking beyond the mountains. At the request of President Jefferson, Meriwether Lewis and William Clark began an expedition in 1804 that eventually explored Oregon, reaching the Pacific in 1805. An American fur trader named John Jacob Astor also entered the region

Meriwether Lewis, American explorer, who, along with William Clark, reached the Pacific in 1805.

[31]

and, in 1811, founded a trading post at Astoria near the mouth of the Columbia River, which Captain Robert Gray had discovered in 1792. Astor, however, was driven out of Oregon during the War of 1812, and thereafter the British-owned Hudson's Bay Company controlled the fur trade in the Pacific Northwest.

Credit for the considerable success of the United States in the four-way contest for Oregon clearly belongs to John Quincy Adams. It was he who in 1818 negotiated a treaty with the British to extend the Canadian-American border from the Great Lakes to the Rocky Mountains along the forty-ninth parallel. He then won their partial admission of American claims to Oregon by including in the agreement a provision for "joint occupation" of the area. The next year in the Florida treaty he eliminated the Spanish claim entirely by obtaining their consent to place the northern boundary of California along the forty-second parallel.

Had the Russians been content with their 1799 claim, which stopped at the fifty-fifth parallel, Adams might not have considered them a menace. But in September, 1821, Czar Alexander I issued a new decree. The trading monopoly of the Russian-American Fur Company was renewed, but this time its exclusive area of operation was pushed south to the fifty-first parallel. Foreign ships were forbidden to come within 100 miles of the shore from that point north to the Bering Strait, and a Russian warship was dispatched to enforce the decree.

Both the British and American governments protested. An indignant John Quincy Adams, in his capacity as secretary of state, raised the issue in cabinet meetings and called for strong countermeasures. Discussions with Russian officials took place throughout 1822 and on into the next year. In June, 1823, Adams

Czar Alexander I of Russia extended the Russian–American Fur Company's area of operation.

[32]

asked that Henry Middleton, the American minister in St. Petersburg, be instructed to tell the Russians that the United States would contest the right of the czar's government to set up any territorial establishment in the Americas. President Monroe and the other members of the cabinet softened this position somewhat, and instructed Middleton to try only to get the Russians to retreat to their older and less expansive claim along the fifty-fifth parallel. Adams could not be persuaded, however, and in time Monroe came to accept his position. Thus, on July 17, 1823, in an interview with Baron von Tuyll, the Russian minister, Adams felt free to note "that we should contest the right of Russia to any territorial establishment on this continent." Significantly, he then added, "and that we should assume distinctly the principle that the American continents are no longer subjects for any new European colonial establishments."

It is not known whether President Monroe reached the same conclusion on his own or had to be converted to this new and far more extensive principle or even realized the significance and implications of the stand that Adams had taken. He did assent to it, however, doing so almost five months before incorporating the point into his famous message to Congress. What does become clearly evident is the concern by the American government with the menace of Russian expansion in North America. In the continent to the south, Americans might have to fight Spaniards supported by Russian advice, prestige, and gold. Along the Pacific coast, there would be no intermediary.

British Relations
with Europe
and America

The most casual student of international affairs in the 1820's could not fail to observe the growing hostility between the United States and the reactionary powers of post-Napoleonic Europe. Equally striking was the fact that once the War of 1812 ended, the relationship between the United States and Great Britain began to improve in spite of a number of incidents that ought to have worsened relations. The primary answer to this paradox was not that the British monarchy had become somewhat more liberal than its Continental neighbors, although it had, or that it was less interested in the future of the Americas, which it was not. Nor was it the result of growing concern with the Concert of Europe, wherein Britain might come to be dominated by a stronger power. The answer, instead, was basically economic.

In the three centuries since such explorers as Columbus had given Spain possession of most of the land and wealth of the Americas, the British had feared and challenged this hegemony. British freebooters had raided the treasure galleons of the Spanish Main; British sea dogs had destroyed the Spanish Armada; and British settlers had planted their British flag in more than a dozen colonies from Canada to the Caribbean. Nothing Madrid could do by force or diplomacy halted the unending struggle of the British to win an increasingly larger share of the enormous wealth pouring out of the New World.

The success of British colonization was extraordinary. From Jamaica to Canada, profits from sugar, cotton, tobacco, furs, naval stores, and other products helped this maritime nation flourish.

Yet, none of the territories originally settled or seized from others were able to produce the huge amounts of precious metal coming from Mexico or Peru. Then, suddenly it mattered less, for thirteen of the colonies disappeared in the American Revolution. Despite this severing of political bonds, it soon became obvious that the economic bonds between the former colonies and the motherland would continue to grow.

Thus, the British were pleased to see the Spanish colonies seek their freedom. Earlier Britain might have considered the possibility of replacing Spain as their master. Now it felt that once independence was won, the colonies would quickly discover, as had the United States, that Britain was the ideal trading partner. Consequently, at the same moment a British army was supporting the Spanish people in their struggle against Napoleon, British gold was being spent to aid the rebellious colonies in Latin America.

Champion of this policy was Robert Banks Jenkinson, second Earl of Liverpool, who served as secretary for war and colonies from 1809 to 1812 and as prime minister from 1812 until 1827. It was Liverpool who directed his nation's efforts against the United States in the War of 1812; yet, at its conclusion, he proposed and supported the moderate Treaty of Ghent, which made the reestablishment of normal relations after the war far easier to achieve. He constantly encouraged the growth of trade between the two nations. In 1818 when General Jackson executed two British subjects, Arbuthnot and Ambrister, Liverpool opposed the demands for war and revenge. He also stood firmly against any effort by the members of the Holy Alliance, with or without French assistance, to aid Ferdinand VII regain his lost empire. On this count at least, Briton and American agreed. Liverpool expected the support of the United States against any power that might try to seize one of these newly freed states. His own nation's trade with Latin America had tripled between 1808 and

1823, and he knew that many American merchants had the same reasons for wanting the ports of these new nations opened to world commerce. In addition, American sympathy for these lately freed colonials gave a second and strongly emotional justification for such support.

Allied to the Earl of Liverpool in these endeavors was Robert Stewart, second Marquis of Londonderry, generally known as Viscount Castlereagh. He served as foreign secretary and leader in the House of Commons from 1812 until his suicide in 1822. A tall, handsome, gifted, and affable aristocrat, he quickly became the dominant figure in the government during this period. Castlereagh spoke for the Prince Regent (George III went blind, and after 1811 was permanently deranged, so his son, who became George IV in 1820, was then acting in his name) at the Congress of Vienna in 1814. There he thwarted the ambitions of both Russia in Poland and Prussia in Saxony by secret treaties with France and Austria. After the Battle of Waterloo in 1815 he secured Napoleon's removal to St. Helena, and opposed Russian, Prussian, and Austrian attempts at further excessive retaliation against France. He executed to the best of his considerable ability the traditional British foreign policy of friendship toward all nations but opposition to any single nation that might become strong enough to dominate the European continent and so threaten the "island kingdom."

For a time in the immediate postwar period, Castlereagh and Metternich of Austria worked together in the Concert of Europe. As Britain came to distrust a reviving France, so Austria worried over the growing power of a warlike and expansionist Russia. The Briton and Austrian parted company, however, when Metternich led the great powers into a policy of suppressing liberalism and revolution in specific countries.

The first great congress of powers since Vienna took place at

Troppau (now the city of Opava in Czechoslovakia) in 1820. There the British dissented from a protocol that denounced states whose governments had been changed by revolution, and proclaimed the right of the powers to use force if necessary to "bring back the guilty state into the bosom of the Great Alliance."

In 1821 a second congress was held at Laibach (now Ljubljana in Yugoslavia). There Ferdinand I of Naples repudiated the oath he had given his people to support a liberal constitution and invited Austrian troops into his kingdom "to restore order," which they promptly did. Again the British were dismayed, and their concern heightened when a call was issued for a third congress to meet at Verona in late 1822. The problem to be discussed was the situation in Spain, where another Ferdinand was for the moment dominated by liberal elements in his own land. Castlereagh worried himself past the breaking point over what might happen, and at this point cut his own throat.

To fill the vacant office of foreign secretary, the Earl of Liverpool chose George Canning. Unlike his predecessor and most high government officials of the day, Canning was a commoner rather than a titled aristocrat. His actress mother and her brother were responsible for his Oxford education. There his brilliance as a scholar led to his rapid rise, and he became in time the chief confidant of Prime Minister William Pitt. After Pitt's death he served as foreign secretary from 1807 to 1810. A year before leaving that office he fought a duel with Castlereagh over the latter's failure to support vigorously Canning's war policy. Then followed twelve years of service in minor posts before he again took over the foreign office, as well as becoming the leader of the House of Commons and the true director of the cabinet as well. Canning finally rose to the highest position of prime minister in 1827.

Of these three key figures, Canning was the man most concerned about policies regarding the American continents. Perhaps this was because he understood more about economics than did Liverpool or Castlereagh, or it may have been that the situation in the New World became more critical at this point than ever before. It is also possible that he was angry enough at what occurred in Verona to concern himself to an increasing extent with an area where he might score a major diplomatic counterblow.

Unlike Castlereagh, Canning, as the new foreign secretary, did not wish to attend the Congress at Verona in person. He persuaded his good friend the Duke of Wellington to go in his stead. Wellington, the conqueror of Napoleon, was a hero throughout Europe, but his advice to the congress was ignored. The reactionaries approved a plan to send a French army into Spain to crush the liberals and their constitution. Ferdinand VII would be restored as an absolute monarch, despite his oath to support the constitution of 1812. Wellington returned home angry and embarrassed. The disappointed Canning busied himself warning the French of the dangers involved in an invasion of Spain, but to no avail. In April, 1823, the French army, under the command of the Duke of Angoulême, took to the field. Madrid fell in May. The liberal ministry fled to Cádiz, which then came under siege from June to October. At that point the liberals surrendered and released the king.

Canning had now suffered another diplomatic defeat. He did not propose to lose again, and it was not difficult to forecast that the next crisis would probably concern the former Spanish possessions in Latin America. No European power appeared to be a likely ally, but across the Atlantic, the United States seemed a strong possibility.

On August 16, 1823, Canning was having a casual conversation on general business matters with Richard Rush, the American minister. Rush happened to mention that his country supported

Britain's opposition to French involvement in Spain, and that should the invasion succeed in its purpose, there was consolation in the knowledge that "Great Britain would not allow her to go farther and stop the progress of emancipation in the colonies." The American minister later reported that Canning replied with a suggestion that the two governments unite in presenting to the world their common feelings on this matter. Canning continued by pointing out that both nations agreed that Spain would never recover its colonies, that their independence must be recognized, and that any attempt to transfer them to another power would not be allowed.

Canning then asked Rush if he had the power to sign such an agreement, in order to prevent "extensive calamities" from taking place. The stunned but tactful and intelligent minister hedged by replying that he had no instructions on the subject. The prime minister asked him to consider the proposal carefully and then left for the country. Rush immediately prepared a report of the conversation for President Monroe. He also answered Canning by letter three days later. In the reply he suggested that further progress was possible provided Great Britain follow the United States in granting immediate recognition to the former Spanish colonies. If this were done, Rush said he was prepared to sign a joint declaration without waiting for approval from Washington.

Canning was not prepared to go quite so far in bringing on an open break with Spain and its allies, but in his answer he still expressed a hope that joint action would be possible. Both men were conscious of the months that had to pass before Rush's dispatches could reach his superiors across the Atlantic, be studied, answered, and returned. Meanwhile, Canning decided to approach

The Duke of Wellington, shown here on his horse Copenhagen at the Battle of Waterloo, attended the congress at Verona.

[41]

the French. Perhaps the posing of a mild threat toward France would succeed. It did, and just as President Monroe was opening two dispatches from Rush, which he found awaiting him on his return to Washington on October 9, 1823, Chateaubriand, the French foreign minister, had prepared an answer to Canning's threats. In it "France disclaimed on her part, any attention or desire to avail herself of the present state of the Colonies, or . . . to appropriate to herself any part of the Spanish possessions in America. . . ." In any case, said Chateaubriand, no action against the colonies would be taken "by force of arms."

Suddenly the pressure on Rush ceased. This, too, could not be known across the Atlantic, where the President and his advisers believed they must quickly establish the most advantageous relationship possible with Great Britain at this time.

The Formation
of a New
American Policy

The city of Washington, D.C., is the capital of the United States, a fact one might have doubted in 1823. Actually, it was then a small southern village, hot, unhealthy, and so lacking in amenities that whenever Congress was not in session, all who could fled elsewhere.

On October 9, a reluctant President James Monroe returned from his farm in Loudoun County, Virginia. He was quickly upset by the contents of the two dispatches from Richard Rush, the American minister in London. When Secretary of State John Quincy Adams arrived from Massachusetts on October 11, the President passed the dispatches along for his study and comment. Monroe then returned to Virginia to consider the problem further. Before leaving, he instructed Adams to have a copy of the dispatches sent to him.

Adams studied carefully the proposals Canning had made to Rush. He quickly saw that there was more here than a simple joint action by the two nations against Spain and its allies. His suspicions were not those of a provincial backwoods American who might have questioned the most innocent proposal of any foreign nation. Rather they sprang from a thorough understanding of the clever and subtle ways of European diplomacy.

John Quincy Adams, son of the second President of the United States, was fifty-six years old. He had spent twenty of those years overseas. As a boy of fourteen he had been sent to St. Petersburg as secretary to the American minister. From 1809 to 1811 he himself was the minister to Russia. In 1814 he helped to

The White House (first known as the President's House), Washington, D.C., during the presidency of James Monroe.

negotiate the Treaty of Ghent, which ended the War of 1812. In 1815 he was made American minister to Great Britain. Since 1817 he had held the position of secretary of state under President Monroe, and his record of achievement in that office remains unsurpassed to this day. Already behind him were the 1818 boundary agreement with the British over Canada and Oregon and the 1819 Florida treaty with Spain. Currently in progress were diplomatic efforts that would result in a treaty with Russia in April, 1824, limiting Russian claims in the northwest to the region above the 50°40′ parallel.

Adams first concluded that the present crisis was an artificial one. He did not believe for a number of reasons that there was any real possibility that France and the other powers would support Spain in an invasion of the Americas. What he did see was Britain, as the stronger half of the proposed partnership, getting most of the credit in Europe and among the Latin Americans for putting an end to the threat of invasion. Even more important than the question of prestige was Canning's suggestion that both countries pledge not to take any Spanish colony for themselves. To Adams that meant Cuba. He knew that both Britain and America considered the island, one of Spain's few remaining possessions, vital in terms of trade and strategic location in the West Indies. The British, if they could not win it for themselves, preferred it in the hands of a weak Spain. For the United States, Adams hoped a better solution might develop. He believed it was only a question of time before the island declared its independence from Spanish rule and would seek union with its northern neighbor. Canning's proposal would prevent that, and so must be opposed. The secretary of state prepared to recommend to the President that the United States reject the offer and act unilaterally.

Meanwhile, President Monroe received the copy of Rush's dispatches. He immediately sent them on to his friend and predecessor Thomas Jefferson, asking his advice and requesting that the dispatches then be forwarded to James Madison, whose opinion he also desired. In the covering letter of October 17, 1823, Monroe's own thinking is clear. He wrote in part:

> *Many important considerations are involved in this proposition. First, shall we entangle ourselves, at all, in European politics and wars on the side of any power, against others, presuming that a concert, by agreement, of the kind proposed, may lead to that result? Second, if a case can exist in which a sound maxim may and ought to be departed from, is not the present instance precisely that case? Third, has not the epoch arrived when Great Britain must take her stand; either on the side of the monarchs of Europe or of the United States and, in consequence, either in favor of despotism or of liberty; and may it not be presumed that, aware of that necessity, her government has seized on the present occurrence as that which it deems the most suitable to announce and mark the commencement of that career?*
>
> *My own impression is that we ought to meet the proposal of the British government and to make it known that we would view an interference on the part of the European powers, and especially an attack on the colonies by them as an attack on ourselves, presuming that, if they succeeded with them, they would extend it to us. I am sensible, however, of the extent and difficulty of the question and shall be happy to have yours and Mr. Madison's opinions on it.*

Jefferson's answer, dated October 24, was definite and to the point. He reminded Monroe that America's "first and fundamental maxim should be never to entangle ourselves in the broils of Europe. Our second, never to suffer Europe to intermeddle in cis-Atlantic affairs." The former President saw Europe as the home of despotism and so the enemy of the Western Hemisphere, which championed freedom. Citing the axiom that one can defeat strong enemies by dividing them and noting the great power of Britain, Jefferson concluded that if "we can effect a division in the body of European powers and draw over to our side its most powerful member, surely we should do it." He agreed with Canning that an Anglo-American declaration would prevent war, and felt that it should state "that we aim not at the acquisition of any of these possessions" and "will not stand in the way of any amicable arrangement between them and the mother country." He added, "We will oppose, with all our means" any forcible settlement and "most especially, their transfer to any power by conquest, cession, or acquisition in any other way."

James Madison's reply to Monroe's request for an opinion was written on October 30. In it he generally supported Jefferson's point of view that a joint declaration with the British was desirable, although he seemed somewhat more suspicious of their motives. He wrote:

> It is particularly fortunate that the policy of Great Britain, although guided by calculations different from ours, has presented a co-operation for an object the same with ours. With that co-operation we have nothing to fear from the rest of Europe; and with it the best reliance on success to our just and laudable views. There ought not be any backwardness therefore, I think, in meeting her in the way she has proposed; keeping in view, of course, the spirit and forms of the Constitution in every step, if those short of war should be without avail.
>
> It cannot be doubted that Mr. Canning's proposal, although made with an air of consultation as well as concert,

was founded on a predetermination to take the course marked out whatever might be the reception given here to his invitation. But this consideration ought not to divert us from what is just and proper in itself. Our co-operation is due to ourselves and to the world. . . .

Then, in a surprising violation of the spirit of neutrality and isolation toward European affairs, which presumably dominated all American thinking since George Washington's day, he added:

Will it not be honorable to our country, and possibly not altogether in vain, to invite the British government to extend the avowed disapprobation of the project against the Spanish colonies to the enterprise of France against Spain herself; and even to join in some declaratory act in behalf of the Greeks?

Here indeed was a novel suggestion of an aggressive foreign policy that would attempt far more than the protection of the Latin American republics from reconquest.

Monroe's hope, if he had any, that all his advisers would advocate a unified policy quickly vanished. He must choose between that given him by his secretary of state and that of two former Presidents, who themselves were not entirely of one mind. On one point, however, there was no disagreement. Adams, six months before in dealing with the Russians, had firmly laid down the policy of no further colonization in the Americas. The foreign policy notes he now gave to the President contained virtually the same words he had used then. Monroe accepted them without change, and the policy was not even discussed at a cabinet meet-

Thomas Jefferson felt that the United States should never entangle itself in Europe's affairs.

[49]

ing. Neither Jefferson nor Madison mentioned the general concept in their letters.

What did receive heated and lengthy attention by the cabinet was the proposed declaration concerning the Latin American question. At least three cabinet members held the view of Jefferson and Madison that a joint statement by the United States and Great Britain was desirable. It took all of John Quincy Adams's powers of persuasion to win the President to the reverse position. Adams argued strongly that there was no true danger from the powers of Europe. They were not nearly as united as might appear at first glance. Then he pointed out that Canning's offer of alliance was to be distrusted. The British government had not yet granted recognition to the former colonies and, if convenient, might change its mind about the American alliance, since at the moment it was not committed. At a cabinet meeting on November 7, Adams suggested that if a formal declaration was considered a necessity, "It will be more candid as well as more dignified to avow our principles explicitly to Russia and France, than to come in as a cock-boat in the wake of the British man-of-war."

The President pondered all this, made his decisions, and presented his views to the world in a speech written for presentation to the first session of the eighteenth Congress on December 2, 1823.

Monroe's Message
to Congress

The Constitution of the United States — in the section dealing with the powers and duties of the President — provides that, "He shall from time to time give to the Congress Information of the State of the Union, and recommend to their Consideration such Measures as he shall judge necessary and expedient. . . ." Out of this provision has come the annual message to Congress, now often referred to as the State of the Union Address and delivered by the President before a joint session of the Congress each January.

Presidents Washington and John Adams delivered their messages in person. The third occupant of the office, Thomas Jefferson, was ill at ease as a public speaker and soon gave up the practice of reading his messages to Congress. He, and all of his successors down to Woodrow Wilson in 1913, preferred to send them in writing.

Many of these annual messages became famous, for in them presidents have often spoken movingly of their hopes and wishes for the country they would lead in the year ahead. Few, however, became as well known as the one Monroe sent to Congress in 1823. Yet, strangely enough, most people today know it not as Monroe's message, but as the Monroe Doctrine, a label it won more than a decade after it was written. Even now it has no legal standing in the United States, never having been enacted into a law, treaty, or convention by the Congress. In fact, the Monroe Doctrine and Monroe's message of December 2, 1823, are not even synonymous.

This seventh annual message from President Monroe covered various aspects of American life. It mentioned the condition of the army, navy, and post office, and discussed the general financial and economic state of the country. It reported on the development of roads and canals. It condemned the slave trade. It noted that there would be a nine-million-dollar surplus in the treasury at the year's end, and suggested that some of it be used to repair the Cumberland Road, then the nation's major highway to the West. The possibility of building a canal to connect Chesapeake Bay with the Ohio River was also included.

A number of paragraphs dealt with foreign affairs. Sympathy was expressed for the cause of the Greek people, then fighting for their independence from the Turks. Another paragraph recommended an international agreement abolishing the practice of privateering.

The actual "Doctrine" appears in parts of two or three paragraphs. Thus, in the opening paragraph, which deals with the negotiations currently in progress with the Russian government over the Pacific Northwest, occurs the statement:

> *In the discussions to which this interest [mutual friendship between Russia and the United States] has given rise, and in the arrangements by which they may terminate, the occasion has been deemed proper for asserting as a principle in which rights and interests of the United States are involved, that the American continents, by the free and independent condition which they have assumed and maintain, are henceforth not to be considered as subjects for future colonization by any European power. . . .*

Above: James Monroe prepared his message to be delivered to Congress on December 2, 1823.
Below: The Pacific Northwest was a subject of concern in Monroe's message to Congress.

[52]

Then, after lengthy concern with domestic matters, Monroe returned to the subject of foreign affairs, writing:

Of events in that quarter of the globe, with which we have so much intercourse and from which we derive our origin, we have always been anxious and interested spectators. The citizens of the United States cherish sentiments the most friendly in favor of the liberty and happiness of their fellow-men on that side of the Atlantic. In the wars of the European powers in matters relating to themselves we have never taken any part, nor does it comport with our policy to do so. It is only when our rights are invaded or seriously menaced that we resent injuries or make preparation for our defense. With the movements in this hemisphere we are of necessity more immediately connected, and by causes which must be obvious to all enlightened and impartial observers. . . . We owe it, therefore, to candor and to the amicable relations existing between the United States and those powers to declare that we should consider any attempt on their part to extend their system to any portion of this hemisphere as dangerous to our peace and safety. With the existing colonies or dependencies of any European power we have not interfered and shall not interfere. But with the Governments who have declared their independence and maintain it, and whose independence we have, on great consideration and on just principles, acknowledged, we could not view any interposition for the purpose of oppressing them or controlling in any other manner their destiny by any European power in any other light than as the manifestation of an unfriendly disposition toward the United States. In the war between those new Governments and Spain we declared our neutrality at the time of their recognition, and to this we have adhered, and shall continue to adhere, provided no change shall occur which, in the judgment of the competent authorities of this Government, shall make a corresponding change on the part of the United States indispensable to their security. . . .

In the next paragraph he continued:

Our policy in regard to Europe, which was adopted at an early stage of the wars which have so long agitated that quarter of the globe, nevertheless remains the same, which is, not to interfere in the internal concerns of any of its powers; to consider the government de facto *as the legitimate government for us; to cultivate friendly relations with it, and to preserve those relations by a frank, firm, and manly policy, meeting in all instances the just claims of every power, submitting to injuries from none. But in regard to those continents circumstances are eminently and conspicuously different. It is impossible that the allied powers should extend their political system to any portion of either continent without endangering our peace and happiness; nor can anyone believe that our southern brethren, if left to themselves, would adopt it of their own accord. It is equally impossible, therefore, that we should behold such interposition in any form with indifference. If we look to the comparative strength and resources of Spain and those new Governments, and their distance from each other, it must be obvious that she can never subdue them. It is still the true policy of the United States to leave the parties to themselves, in the hope that other powers will pursue the same course. . . .*

The Monroe Doctrine thus expresses two general principles. In the first, it proclaims the American continents closed to any further colonization. In the second, it points out that the political system and the philosophy of the European continent are different from that of the Americas, and that good relations in the future can only be based on an appreciation of that fact. Any attempt on the part of the reactionary powers in Europe to extend their system to any part of the New World would be firmly opposed by the United States.

These two ideas — no further colonization in America and the separation of the Western Hemisphere from the domination and control of Europe — are the essential parts of the Monroe Doctrine. The first has caused relatively little controversy, being a simple statement of opposition to a practice easily identifiable. The arrival of a foreign fleet and army in the New World landing on the coast of a self-proclaimed independent nation would be easily understood by all Americans.

The second idea was more sophisticated and, therefore, harder to identify and deal with than armies and navies. Absolute differences between the nations in the two hemispheres were obviously difficult to establish. Not every government in Europe was a despotism, and those that were did not have the support of all their citizens. On the other hand, not every new Latin American government practiced democracy or was even a republic. Moreover, a counterpromise made to Europe was open to various interpretations. The United States promised to continue what it claimed was a well-established policy of noninterference in strictly internal European affairs. This was an extension of the doctrine of neutrality and isolation first practiced by Washington in the days when he warned his countrymen "to steer clear of permanent alliances with any portion of the foreign world." It was confirmed by Jefferson in his inaugural address when he spoke out against "entangling alliances." Finally, this second idea involved a vague pledge that the United States itself would refrain

[56]

from interfering in the internal affairs of the Latin American nations.

It was soon obvious that President Monroe's unilateral declaration created a number of difficult questions and problems for his countrymen. What would happen if the European powers called America's bluff? How far could the United States go in cooperating with the British before it became involved in a permanent and entangling alliance? Was a denunciation of the despotic regimes governing most of Europe to be called interference in that Continent's internal affairs? What would happen if one of the independent Latin American nations instituted a policy of repression or of trade restrictions that went counter to the beliefs held by the United States? The public proclamation of these principles would cause much concern among thinking citizens and responsible leaders for decades to come.

Conclusion

The United States in 1823 was in no position to enforce or defend the stand taken by President Monroe in his message to Congress. Fortunately for him, the issue proved to be academic. British policy, backed up by the greatest navy in the world, constituted an insurmountable barrier to the Continental powers. In any case, the President's words were ignored or scorned by European statesmen. Only the British were at all concerned with American policy, and their disappointment over the United States's refusal to agree to a joint declaration was a minor one. They realized that unilateral action by both countries could still move in the same direction and be effective. At the moment communications between the two nations were excellent, so that there was still a strong possibility for a more unified policy in the future. Besides, the looming crisis had already been settled privately. Canning had been assured that France would take no action against the former Spanish colonies, and without its aid Spain was too poor and weak to act alone.

Of considerable importance to students of history is the debate that still rages over whose ideas were best expressed in the speech. Historians almost unanimously concede that the idea, and even the words, concerning the ban on new colonization came from John Quincy Adams. They strenuously disagree about the circumstances that gave rise to the new policy, what its purpose was, why it was proclaimed in 1823, and what it was expected to accomplish.

Dexter Perkins, who wrote the first major study of the Monroe Doctrine, saw it chiefly aimed at blocking the Russians in the Pacific Northwest and the Continental powers in Latin America. Edward H. Tatum, Jr., saw its main purpose as dif-

Most historians credit John Quincy Adams with the ideas in the Monroe Doctrine concerning the ban on new colonization.

fusing a potential threat from the British by joining them in alliance against the other European powers. Arthur P. Whitaker insisted that in the immediate circumstances it was directed against the French, who alone were actually considering concrete action.

When attempting to establish authorship of the ideas in the Doctrine, further disputes occur. Worthington C. Ford, who edited the writings of John Quincy Adams in seven volumes, gives him most of the credit. T. R. Schellenberg stresses the role played by Thomas Jefferson, and William A. MacCorkle favors James Madison. An eminent British historian, C. K. Webster, even makes a responsible case for George Canning as the author.

Such serious differences of opinion and interpretation show beyond any doubt that the Monroe Doctrine could and would be twisted and shaped in the decades that followed 1823. Some of the changes were added in the form of numerous corollaries by Presidents Polk, Grant, Cleveland, and Theodore Roosevelt. Some were minor and caused little stir in diplomatic circles. Others, such as the corollary proclaimed by President Roosevelt in 1904, were major. That particular corollary asserted the right of the United States to intervene forcibly in the affairs of Latin American nations whenever they engaged in "chronic wrongdoing." It resulted in a serious strain on the relations between the United States and its southern neighbors for a quarter of a century, until renounced in 1928.

In the past any threat of an invasion of the Americas by foreign powers brought forth almost unanimous cries of anger from the people and leaders of the United States. That part of the Monroe Doctrine still remains a landmark in the foreign policy of the nation. The sections dealing with the differences in political systems between the Old and New World are no longer valid and have faded away. The American pledge to stand apart from the internal affairs and wars of Europe has almost totally been destroyed by two world wars, and a common fear of Communist expansion has bound most of the Continent and the United States in agreements, such as the North Atlantic Treaty, which remain in force today.

Even the section of the Monroe Doctrine that is still generally accepted may be out of date and meaningless. Secret internal subversion rather than open military invasion seems to be the approach being used in the last half of the twentieth century. No Russian flag flies over a Cuba ruled by Fidel Castro, yet it could be argued that it is a "colony" in all but name.

In any case, a basic reason for a Monroe Doctrine is fast disappearing. The states of Latin America are no longer weak and insignificant members of the society of nations. They no longer need and want — if they ever did — American political and economic domination. To the extent that domination still exists, it is now being challenged not by foreign powers, but by the Latin Americans themselves.

Beyond any sentimental, philosophic, humanitarian, or political importance it may have, one fundamental fact remains. Perhaps unconsciously in many cases, Americans of all persuasions relate the Monroe Doctrine with the security of their nation. That is why its evolution through the past century and a half has been of major concern, and why its final repudiation in the future would be a sign of one of the greatest shifts in the history of American foreign policy.

Bibliography

The following works have been helpful in the writing of this book and will be of assistance to any reader who wishes to probe deeper into the subject.

Bemis, Samuel Flagg. *John Quincy Adams and the Foundation of American Foreign Policy.* New York: Knopf, 1949.

Cresson, W. P. *The Holy Alliance: The European Background of the Monroe Doctrine.* New York: Carnegie Endowment of International Peace, 1922.

Dangerfield, George. *The Awakening of American Nationalism 1815–1828.* New York: Harper Row, 1965.

Donovan, Frank. *Mr. Monroe's Message: The Story of the Monroe Doctrine.* New York: Dodd, Mead, 1963.

Ford, Worthington C. *John Quincy Adams and the Monroe Doctrine.* New York: Amer. Historical Review, VIII, 1902.

MacCorkle, W. A. *The Personal Genesis of the Monroe Doctrine.* New York: G. P. Putnam's Sons, 1923.

Perkins, Dexter. *Hands Off: A History of the Monroe Doctrine.* Boston: Little, Brown, 1941.

———— *The Monroe Doctrine 1823–1826.* Cambridge: Harvard University Press, 1927. The single best work on the subject.

Schellenberg, T. R. *Jeffersonian Origins of the Monroe Doctrine.* New York: Hispanic Amer. Historical Review, XIV, 1934.

Tatum, Edward L. *The United States and Europe 1815–1823.* Baltimore: University of California Press, 1936.

Webster, Charles K. *The Foreign Policy of Castlereagh 1815–1822.* London: Hillary, 1963.

Whitaker, Arthur Preston. *The United States and the Independence of Latin America.* Baltimore: The Johns Hopkins Press, 1941.

Index

About the Author

The Monroe Doctrine is a familiar subject to Harold Cecil Vaughan. A student and teacher of history over the past twenty-five years, he has been on the faculty of the Collegiate School in New York City and the Brooklyn Friends School, and now teaches at the Ridgewood High School in New Jersey. A native New Yorker, he served in the Army Air Corps after receiving his A.B. degree from Columbia College, and returned to Columbia University for his M.A. and further graduate study. He is an avid fan of the legitimate theater and his alma mater's football team. Mr. Vaughan is a frequent lecturer on historical subjects to the National Society of the Colonial Dames in New York and has been a guest speaker to the Junior League, the Long Island Historical Association, and the Contemporary Club. His previous Focus Books include *The Citizen Genêt Affair*, *The Hayes-Tilden Election of 1876* and *The XYZ Affair*.

DATE DUE

DEC 17 '76			